ARCTIC OCEAN
SEVERNAYA ZEMLYA
FRANZ JOSEF
NEW SIBERIAN ISLANDS
NOVAYA ZE
Wrangel Island
FINLAND
RUSSIA
ESTONIA
LATVIA
LITHUANIA
BELARUS
UKRAINE
MOLDOVA
ROMANIA
BULGARIA
GREECE
TURKEY
GEORGIA
ARMENIA
AZERBAIJAN
KAZAKHSTAN
UZBEKISTAN
TURKMENISTAN
KRYGYSTAN
TAJIKISTAN
MONGOLIA
CHINA
NORTH KOREA
SOUTH KOREA
JAPAN
NORTH PACIFIC OCEAN
CYPRUS
SYRIA
IRAQ
IRAN
AFGHANISTAN
PAKISTAN
JORDAN
KUWAIT
NEPAL
BHUTAN
BANGLADESH
EGYPT
SAUDI ARABIA
QATAR
UNITED ARAB EMIRATES
OMAN
YEMEN
INDIA
MYANMAR (BURMA)
LAOS
THAILAND
VIETNAM
CAMBODIA
PHILIPPINES
GUAM
FEDERATED STATES OF MICRONESIA
MARSHALL ISLANDS
SUDAN
ERITREA
DJIBOUTI
ETHIOPIA
SOMALIA
ADAMAN ISLANDS (INDIA)
NICOBAR ISLANDS (INDIA)
MALDIVES
SRI LANKA
MALAYSIA
BRUNEI
CENTRAL AFRICAN REPUBLIC
DEM. REP. OF THE CONGO
UGANDA
KENYA
RWANDA
BURUNDI
TANZANIA
SEYCHELLES
INDONESIA
PAPUA NEW GUINEA
SOLOMON ISLANDS
KIRIBATI
TUVALU
SAMOA
COMOROS
MALAWI
ZAMBIA
MOZAMBIQUE
ZIMBABWE
BOTSWANA
MADAGASCAR
MAURITIUS
REUNION
INDIAN OCEAN
VANUATU
FIJI
TONGA
NEW CALEDONIA (FRANCE)
AUSTRALIA
SWAZILAND
SOUTH AFRICA
LESOTHO
NEW ZEALAND
TASMANIA (AUSTRALIA)
PRINCE EDWARD ISLANDS
ILES CROZET (FRANCE)
KERGUELEN ISLAND (FRANCE)

GLOBETROTTERS
INDIA
Jane Hinchey
REDBACK
publishing

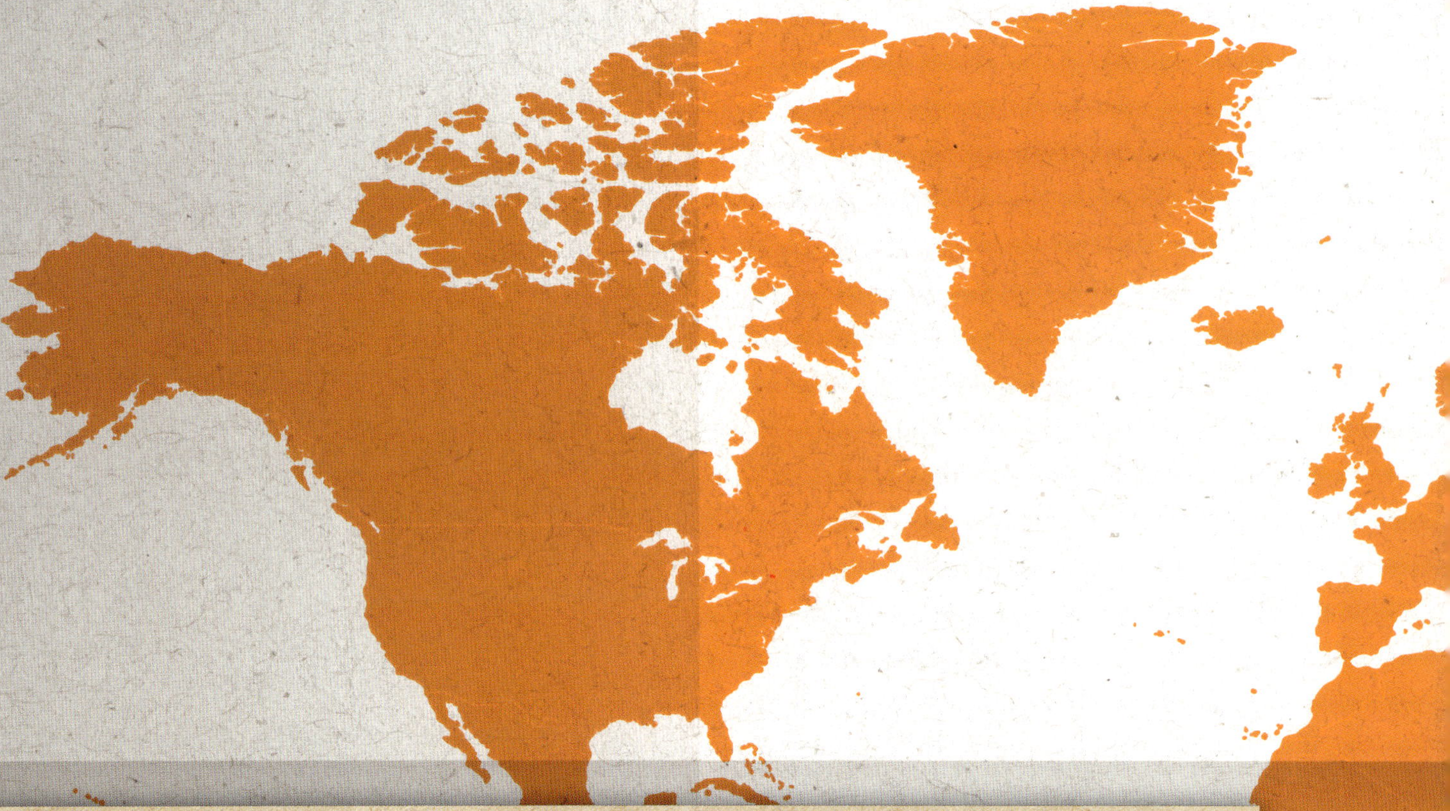

First Published 2022 by
Redback Publishing
PO Box 357 Frenchs Forest NSW 2086
Australia

www.redbackpublishing.com
orders@redbackpublishing.com

ISBN 978-1-922322-95-1 HBK

Author: Jane Hinchey
Editor: Marlene Vaughan
Design: Redback Publishing

Original illustrations © Redback Publishing 2022
Originated by Redback Publishing

Printed and bound in Malaysia

Acknowledgements
Abbreviations: l—left, r—right, b—bottom, t—top, c—centre, m—middle
We would like to thank the following for permission to reproduce photographs: (Images © shutterstock, wikimediacommons) p4bl Catalin Lazar, p5tl Amit kg, p6bl Tingling1, p7tr Jayakumar, p8tl Amit.pansuriya, p9bl Mazur Travel, p9cl Harshit Dhiman, p10cl stockpexel, p11tr Sonia Dhankhar, p11cr PradeepGaurs, p12tl CherylRamalho, p13cl PIXATHON, p14tr Snehal Jeevan Pailkar, p14bl Memoryfor, p16br Yury Birukov, p17br Sahil Ghosh, p18tr reddees, p18cl Rudra Narayan Mitra, p19tr OmMishra, p19cl Denis Makarenko, p20tl Soban (https://commons.wikimedia.org/wiki/File:Priest_King_Monument.jpg), p21tr Public domain (https://commons.wikimedia.org/wiki/File:Gandhi_smiling.jpg), p21cl Public domain (https://commons.wikimedia.org/wiki/File:Lord_Mountbatten_meets_Nehru,_Jinnah_and_other_Leaders_to_plan_Partition_of_India.jpg), p21br rook76, p22tr Mahesh M J, p24bl Matyas Rehak, p25tr CherylRamalho, p27bl Pratikkumar Bhatt, p28tr Malcolm P Chapman, p30tr Ministry of Home Affairs, Public domain (https://commons.wikimedia.org/wiki/File:Emblem_of_India.svg), p30cl reddees

Every effort has been made to contact copyright holders of any material reproduced in this book. Any omissions will be rectified in subsequent printings if notice is given to the publisher.

A catalogue record for this book is available from the National Library of Australia

CONTENTS

MAP OF INDIA

Golden Temple
AMRITSAR, PUNJAB

Taj Mahal
AGRA, UTTAR PRADESH

New Delhi

Mumbai

Lotus Temple
NEW DEHLI

Key Monastery
HIMACHAL PRADESH

India Gate
NEW DELHI

Agra Fort (The Red Fort of Agra)
AGRA, UTTAR PRADESH

SNAPSHOT

COUNTRY
Republic of India

CAPITAL
New Delhi

OFFICIAL LANGUAGES
Hindi, English

AREA
3,287,236 square kilometres

POPULATION
1,395,568,473 (2021)

HIGHEST POINT Puncak Jaya, 4,884 metres

RELIGIONS Hinduism, Islam, Buddhism, Christianity, Sikhism, Jainism

CURRENCY ₹ Indian rupee

GOVERNMENT Sovereign Socialist Secular Democratic Republic

Did You Know?

India has the second largest English speaking population in the world, with 125 million English speakers.

WELCOME TO INDIA

Local women carrying water jugs on their heads

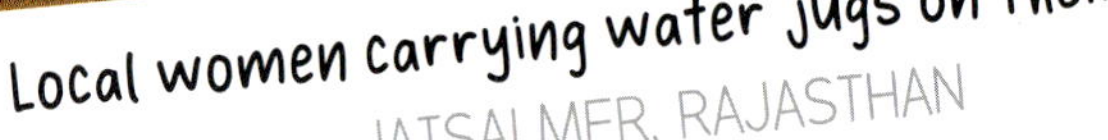

JAISALMER, RAJASTHAN

Himalayan Mountains

India is a land of contrasts. Each region has distinct landforms, vegetation and climate. It boasts some of the world's most beautiful scenery, from soaring mountains and high plateaux to vast deserts and low-lying plains and rivers.

Aerial view of New Delhi from the Masjid-i Jehan-Numa

India's capital city is New Delhi, a sprawling mega city that has developed around Old Delhi, the historical heart of the city. In 2021, India had 40 UNESCO World Heritage Sites, ranking sixth in the world in this category. Many of these sites make up the country's most important tourist destinations.

India is the world's largest democracy and has the world's fastest growing economy. It is the second most populated country in the world, exceeding 1.39 billion in 2021. The country is divided into 28 different states and eight union territories. Each state has their own traditions, languages and ways of life. There are many native languages spoken amongst many different ethnic groups and different customs between villages.

Shopping mall in chennai
TAMIL NADU

India's 28 States

1. Andhra Pradesh
2. Arunachal Pradesh
3. Assam
4. Bihar
5. Chhattisgarh
6. Goa
7. Gujarat
8. Haryana
9. Himachal Pradesh
10. Jharkhand
11. Karnataka
12. Kerala
13. Madhya Pradesh
14. Maharashtra
15. Manipur
16. Meghalaya
17. Mizoram
18. Nagaland
19. Odisha
20. Punjab
21. Rajasthan
22. Sikkim
23. Tamil Nadu
24. Telangana
25. Tripura
26. Uttarakhand
27. Uttar Pradesh
28. West Bengal

AT A GLANCE

Narendra Modi - Prime minister of India 2021

Government

India is a Sovereign, Socialist, Secular, Democratic Republic that has a parliamentary system of government. The President of India is the Head of State, while the Prime Minister of India acts as an advisor to the President and is the leader of the Council of Ministers. The President of India is elected for five years. The President can choose the Prime Minister.

Top Exports

India's top exports include refined petroleum, diamonds, medicines and therapeutic goods, jewellery and cars.

Top Imports

India's top imports include crude petroleum, coal briquettes, gold, diamonds and telephones.

Main Agriculture

India is the world's largest producer of pulses, rice, wheat, spices and spice products, and is the second largest fruit producer in the world.

Spices on display at Anjuna Market in Goa

India has the second-largest area of arable land in the world

Natural Resources

India has the fourth-largest reserves of coal in the world. Other natural resources include natural gas, chromite, iron ore, manganese, mica, limestone, bauxite, rare earth elements, titanium ore, diamonds, petroleum, and arable land.

The Sari

A variety of traditional clothes have developed over time in India, all influenced by region, culture, religion and climate. The most famous of India's traditional outfits is the sari. Worn by women, a sari is a piece of cloth that is draped over the body in various styles. They range from everyday plain dyed cotton to ornate silks for special occasions.

DAILY LIFE

Family is the focus of daily life in India. Families are large and it is common to live with two or more generations, especially in rural areas where many generations help run farms. In cities, grandparents help care for young children, so their parents can work.

Families are patriarchal, meaning the head of the family is male and makes all major decisions, including what career paths the children will take and who they will marry. Most marriages are arranged by the families of the bride and groom. Sometimes the families use the services of a professional matchmaker.

Hindu Caste System

Hindu people are born into social groups, known as castes. The caste system has four main categories:

- Brahmins (priests, academics)
- Kshatriyas (military, rulers)
- Vaishyas (merchants, tradesmen, farmers)
- Shudras (artisans, labourers, service providers)

Brahmins

Kshatriyas

Vaishyas

Shudras

Dalits (Untouchables)

Outside of the Hindu caste system are the Dalits, also known as the untouchables. The untouchables have always been considered the lowest in society. Since 1947, the Indian Constitution has forbidden discrimination but it is still difficult to rise above this social ranking.

EDUCATION

Children in India can attend primary school from age six to twelve. High school caters for students up to age 18. About 20 per cent of children don't attend school, with the majority of these coming from poor families. Only 40 per cent of children attend high school, most of whom are from wealthy families. The Indian government provides free education to girls over 14 years in a bid to keep them in school. For children from wealthier families, there is a lot of pressure to do well in school. Many Indians attend technical college or university once they have completed school. India has the third largest higher education system, after China and the US.

LANGUAGE

There are 22 official languages in India with 44 per cent of the population speaking Hindi. There are also over 1,600 different dialects, and 29 Indian languages have over a million speakers per language. English is spoken widely and is used in business and government circles.

Learn the Lingo: Hindi

Namaste
Hello

Haan
Yes

Alavida
Goodbye

Nahin
No

Krpya
Please

Dhanyavad
Thank you

SPORT

Keen cricketers play in the snow at Key Monastery, Himachal Pradesh

India is a nation that takes sport very seriously. While hockey is the official national sport, cricket is the country's most popular sport. All over India, in every city and every village, people play cricket. Introduced to India by the British during colonial times, cricket players are treated like rock stars. There are many cricket stadiums around the country. Poorer people will watch games on television. Even those people who don't have their own television will find one nearby for important matches.

Other popular sports include polo, tennis and soccer.

Sachin Tendulkar, India's God of Cricket

Sachin Ramesh Tendulkar is a former international cricketer and a former captain of the Indian national team. He is the highest run scorer of all time in International cricket, regarded as one of the greatest batsmen of all time. Admired all around the cricket world, he is elevated to god-like status in India.

RELIGION

Religion is the foundation of India's culture and daily life. Three of the world's major religions, Buddhism, Hinduism and Sikhism began in India.

Hinduism is the most widely practised religion, making up about 80 per cent of the population.

In India all religions are given equal status by law. There are some religious tensions, but generally Indian people are tolerant of the different faiths.

Thousands of Hindu devotees in Mumbai with a statue of Ganesha at the Ganesh Chaturthi Festival

Hinduism

Hinduism developed around 4,000 years ago. There is no single founder, and no specific set of teachings. While there is belief in a single supreme being, followers worship many deities, or gods.

- Ganesha: This beloved deity has the head of an elephant. Hindus consider him the Remover of Obstacles and ask for his assistance on all matters in life.
- Lakshmi: This is the goddess of good fortune, wealth and well-being.

Sacred Cows

Cows are considered to be sacred, so Hindus don't eat beef. It is not uncommon to see cows wandering the streets in India.

Buddhism

In the fifth century BC, a prince called Siddhattha Gautama turned his back on his life of privilege and went on a spiritual journey. This led to the birth of one of the world's great religions, Buddhism. Despite being founded in India and being embraced all around the world, the Buddhist population of India is relatively small.

Statue of Lord Buddha
RAVANGLA, SIKKIM

Palitana Jain Temples
BHAVNAGAR DISTRICT, GUJARAT

Islam

Islam is the second most common religion in India. Muslims believe in one god, called Allah, who gave his message to a prophet called Mohammed. The holy book is called the Koran. Ramadan is the most important event on the Islamic calendar.

Jainism

Jains believe they must live a pure life. To do so they practice:

- Non-violence
- Truth
- Non-stealing
- Chastity
- Non-attachment

Sikhism

The Sikh religion began around 600 years ago and now has over 25 million followers worldwide. Sikhs believe in one god, reincarnation and that everyone is equal.

LIFE IN CITIES

India has 40 cities with a population of more than one million people. Mumbai, Delhi and Kolkata and their outer regions are known as mega cities.

India's cities are noisy, polluted and densely populated. But they also have world-class facilities, restaurants and shopping centres, and life for the more fortunate can be exciting and cosmopolitan. Wealthy people live in gated seclusion, in beautiful homes, with servants and drivers. India has a growing middle class and these families also live in comfort, with hired help. Others live in high-rise apartments, in new residential areas. Wealthier Indians have the opportunity to be well-educated and have good careers.

Mumbai at dusk

However many people live in poverty. Over 100 million residents live in urban slums. In these slums, the streets are narrow and often sewage water runs into open drains. Some areas lack basic sanitation services, and often have no access to electricity or clean water.

LIFE IN RURAL AREAS

Almost 70 per cent of India's population still lives in towns and villages, or in the countryside. There are around 700,000 villages in India. More than half of India's population is employed in farming. Fishing is another a major industry.

Life in the countryside can be tough. Some places are difficult to get to, so relationships with neighbours are important. How difficult life is depends on whether you're rich or poor, as well as what caste you were born into. Wealthy people in the countryside live in two storey houses, with running water, electricity and servants, but the majority of rural dwellers live in small mud or straw shacks. These villagers often have to walk miles each day to access clean drinking water. Education is often seen as a luxury and many children leave school early to help on their family farms. Other infrastructure, such as roads and access to health care, is limited.

Farmer's house in Jaisalmer, Rajasthan

Villagers often have to travel far to access clean drinking water

THE ARTS

Artwork on a Hindu temple in Hyderabad

Indian culture stretches back thousands of years, with rich art forms developing over time. The first sculptures in India date back to the Indus Valley civilisation 5,000 years ago. The arrival of religions such as Hinduism, Buddhism and Jainism further influenced art forms.

Today, music, theatre, art and literature are enjoyed as much as ever, but the most popular of all the art forms is film.

Artwork based on the epic Mahabharata poem
KOLKATA, WEST BENGAL

Great Tales

Indian people love a grand tale. India's history is awash with famous stories of revenge, war and most importantly, love. The earliest works of literature were epics, long poems, travelogues, plays, and verse. The two most famous epics are the Mahabharata and the Ramayana.

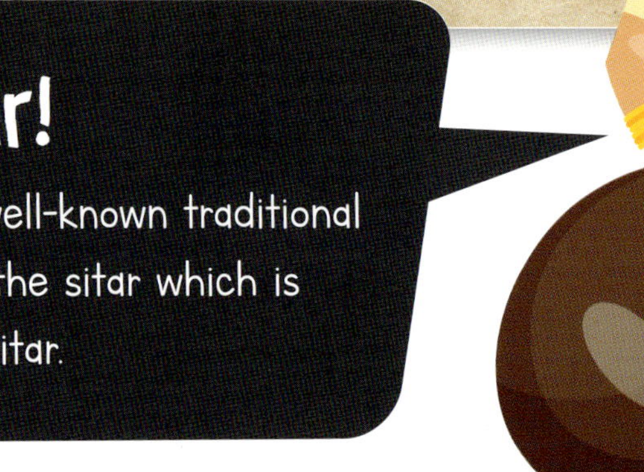

Air Sitar!

India's most well-known traditional instrument is the sitar which is similar to a guitar.

Bollywood

India's film industry, known as Bollywood, is the largest in the world. Bollywood studios produce over 1,000 films annually. Over 22 billion movie tickets are sold each year in India, twice the amount of China in second place. About 14 million people go to the cinema every day.

Bollywood films involve a lot of drama, action and romance. Another key component is song and dance. Dance numbers are especially important between the hero and heroine. The dance-form used in films is a mixture of styles such as Indian folk dance, belly dancing and modern dance. Bollywood dance styles have become famous around the world.

Bollywood star Shah Rukh Khan

There are many famous actors, but the undisputable King of Bollywood is Shah Rukh Khan. In India he is known as King Khan, or SRK. He has starred in over 100 films and is one of the most successful actors in the world.

Two Great Bollywood Films for Kids

- *Taare Zameen Par*: An inspiring film about a dyslexic boy.
- *Jajantaram Mamantaram*: A film inspired by Gulliver's Travels.

KEY MOMENTS IN HISTORY

Four thousand years ago, a highly advanced civilisation lived in a sophisticated city in the Indus Valley

Indus Valley Civilisation

One of the world's oldest civilisations was in India. The Indus Valley Civilisation began in northwest India around 2600 BC. Indus Valley cities were well-planned, very advanced and included plumbing, trade routes and innovative agricultural methods.

Ashoka and the Mauryan Empire

Ashoka the Great was emperor of the Maurya Dynasty which ruled the Indian subcontinent from 269 BC to 232 BC. Known to be a cruel leader, he later changed and built many hospitals and universities, and treated his subjects as equals, regardless of their religion, politics and caste.

Mughal Empire

The Mughal Empire was founded in 1526 by Babur, a descendant of Genghis Khan. Babur and the successive Mughal rulers built great cities and oversaw important works of art, such as the Taj Mahal.

From British Rule to Independence

The British ruled the Indian subcontinent from the late 18th century until 1947, when India's independence movement succeeded. A key leader of India's independence movement was Mohandas Gandhi. Gandhi used nonviolent methods to protest against British rule. His efforts earned him the title Mahatma, which means 'great soul.'

Mahatma Gandhi

Lord Mountbatten, the last Viceroy of India, meets with other leaders to plan the Partition of India

As the British withdrew from colonial India, they partitioned the country based on religion. Over the next two decades, approximately 15 million people were forced to migrate up to 1,500 kilometres – often on foot. Hindus and Sikhs were forced into India and Muslims were forced to Pakistan. It was one of the largest forced migrations in history and it left up to two million people dead.

A Great Stateswoman

Indira Gandhi was Prime Minister twice. She was the daughter of India's first Prime Minister, Jawaharlal Nehru, and the mother of another Prime Minister, Rajiv Gandhi. Indira Gandhi was one of India's most remarkable political leaders after independence. She was assassinated on October 31, 1984.

FOOD

Indian food is so common in the west that it can be surprising just how diverse it is. Indian cuisine has developed over time and is influenced by geography, weather, access to ingredients and ethnic groups. The country's main religions also employ different dietary restrictions.

Southern Indian food is hot and eaten with chillies and rice, while northern cuisine is less spicy and served with flat bread such as parathas and chapatis.

Street food vendors in Old Delhi

Most regions use an array of spices. Staples include lentils, chickpeas, rice, yoghurt, onion, garlic and turmeric, aromatic herbs and spices, and ghee.

The most important meal of the day is dinner, which families eat together. Numerous dishes are served, from which you help yourself. Meals usually comprise of rice, chapati, meat, vegetable and lentil dishes, salad, yogurt and pickles. While people do use cutlery, it is also common to eat using your fingers.

Etiquette Alert!

Do not use your left hand to eat! Indians consider the left hand to be unclean. (It's the hand they use when they go to the toilet.) This probably makes life difficult for people who are naturally left-handed.

ON THE MENU

Dishes from Northern India

Aloo Gobi

Sautéed cauliflower and potatoes, with garam masala, turmeric and curry leaves.

Chicken Tikka Masala

Chicken marinated in spicy yogurt and tomato sauce.

Daal

Popular lentil and spice dish.

Naan Roti

Baked soft flatbread.

Palak Paneer

Pieces of paneer (a fresh crumbly cheese) in a spinach curry.

Samosa

Potatoes, onions, peas, coriander and lentils in pastry triangles.

Dosa

Chicken Tikka Masala

Vada

Tandoori Chicken

Marinated, roasted chicken with spices and yoghurt.

Dishes from Southern India

Dosa

A type of savoury pancake.

Papadams

Thin deep fried crisp made of flour, lentils or chickpeas and eaten as a starter to a meal.

Kuzhakkattai

Vegetarian sweet dumplings.

Vada

Savory snack made from lentil and gram flour, often eaten with chutney.

India is a peninsula, surrounded on three sides by water. In the west is the Arabian Sea, in the south is the Indian Ocean and in the east is the Bay of Bengal. It shares borders with Pakistan, Bangladesh, Myanmar, China, Bhutan and Nepal.

GEOGRAPHY AND CLIMATE

View of the Himalayas near Sonamarag in the Ganderbal district of Jammu and Kashmir

Mountain Ranges

Northern India is mountainous, with eight important mountain ranges. The most famous mountain range in India is the Himalayas, which runs across the top of India and into Nepal and China. The mountains are covered in snow and there are farmlands in the valleys.

Monsoon rains cause a flooded street in Varanasi, Uttar Pradesh

Climate

India has a number of different climates. In the South, the climate is tropical, and it gets very hot in summer and cooler in winter. The western deserts are hot and dry. Northern India is sub-tropical, while its mountainous regions have alpine climates. The Himalayas get extremely cold. India gets monsoon rain that sweeps across the country for three months of the year.

Caravan of camels in Jaisalmer, Rajasthan

Hindus partake in the religious ritual of bathing in the Ganges River

The Great Ganges

The Ganges River is greatly respected as a God. It rises in the Himalayas and flows 2,495 kilometres east to the Bay of Bengal. Human development has replaced all the original natural vegetation with cultivated farmland or urban development. The Ganges supports one of the densest populations on Earth and has become severely polluted. It's source glacier, Gangotri Glacier, has also been impacted by climate change.

Desert Region

The Thar Desert, also known as the Great Indian Desert, covers an area of 238,000 square kilometres between India and Pakistan. More than 60 per cent of the desert lies in the state of Rajasthan, home to some of India's most famous cities and historical sites. The desert is covered with shifting sand dunes and salt lakes that fill with water during monsoon season.

Indo-Gangetic Plain

The Indo-Gangetic Plain is a rich, fertile area of 2.5 million kilometres, encompassing most of northern and eastern India. The area is named after the Ganges River and the Indus River, two of the extensive river systems that weave across this region. Many of India's largest cities are located in the region, including New Delhi, Kolkata, Jaipur, and Varanasi. It is one of the most intensely farmed regions in the world.

FABULOUS FLORA & FAUNA

India's rich flora habitats range from deciduous forests and thick tropical jungles to cool temperate woods. There are tropical forests in the east and pine and coniferous woodlands in the western Himalayas. The Himalayan foothills are home to deciduous trees and shrubs, bamboos, ferns and grasses, while the Indo-Gangetic plain provides a diverse range of habitats. These are all home to a rich variety of creatures.

Blue poppies (*Papaver guilelmi-waldemarii*), Valley of Flowers National park, Uttarakhand

While much of India's natural world has been destroyed during the country's rapid development, there is a growing trend towards environmentalism to maintain and save what's left. To protect wildlife, India now has 104 national parks covering an area of 43,716 square kilometres.

Bengal tiger (*Panthera tigris tigris*) on the lake shore in Ranthambore National Park

Asian elephant bathing on the southern banks of the Periyar River, Kerala

There are over 500 species of mammals in India, 200 species of birds and over 30,000 species of insects. Animals such as the Asian elephant, lion, Royal Bengal Tiger and Indian Bison all call India home, as well as numerous species of leopards, deer and monkey.

The Snow Leopard (Panthera uncia) is native to the Himalayas

However some of India's exotic animals are close to extinction, including:

- Nilgiri Tahr
- Bengal Tigers
- Asiatic Lion
- Blackbuck
- Lion Tailed Macaque

Blackbuck jumping at Thol Bird sanctuary, Gujarat

TRANSPORT

India is a large country with a huge population and diverse geography. Improvements to transport infrastructure are continuing in India and the public transport systems are crowded. Popular modes of alternative transport include human-pulled or motorised rickshaws, bicyles and walking.

Commuters travel to work on a motorised rickshaw near Dhrangadhra, Gujarat

Did You Know?

Indian Railway employs 1.3 million people, making it the single largest employer on the planet.

Railways

First built during British rule, India's rail network is now the most heavily used rail network on the planet. Every day over 20,000 trains carry three million tonnes of goods and over 23 million people across vast distances.

TAJ MAHAL

Taj Mahal – One of the Seven New Wonders of the World

India's most famous tourist attraction, and its beloved crown jewel is the Taj Mahal. The Taj Mahal is a mausoleum of white marble in Agra, Uttar Pradesh. Ruler of the Mughal Empire, Shah Jahan, had the mausoleum constructed to honour his favourite wife, Mumtaz Mahal, after her death in 1631.

Taj Mahal literally means 'the crown of palaces'. Over 22,000 labourers and 1,000 elephants worked for 22 years to complete it. Masons, inlayers, carvers, painters, and other artisans were brought from as far away as Iran to work on it. A total of 43 different precious and semi precious stones were used to decorate it. It is one of the most beautiful buildings in the world, and India's top tourist attraction.

Marble window inlay at the Taj Mahal

Detail of inlay decorating the Taj Mahal

FLAG, SYMBOLS AND EMBLEMS

The National Emblem

The State Emblem of India is a replica of the Lion Capital of Ashoka in Sarnath, near Varanasi in Uttar Pradesh. It depicts four lions standing back to back and stands for power, courage and confidence.

School children in Hyderabad assemble with a giant Indian flag to perform the national anthem

National Anthem

Jana Gana Mana is the national anthem of India.

Flag of India

India's flag has three horizontal colours in equal proportion. The colours are deep saffron on the top, white in the middle and dark green at the bottom.

Deep saffron represents courage and sacrifice. White stands for peace, unity and truth. Green symbolises faith and fertility.

In the centre of the flag is a blue wheel called the Dharmachakra, or 'Wheel of Law' The Dharmachakra represents the progress of the nation and the importance of justice. The blue represents the sky and the ocean.

The flag was adopted on July 22, 1947, after India became independent from Great Britain.

National Bird

Indian peacock

National Flower

Lotus

National Tree

Indian Banyan

National Animal

Royal Bengal tiger

GLOSSARY

Buddhism religion based on the teachings of Buddha

caste social group into which Hindus are born

climate change shift in the planet's weather and climate patterns

culture practices, beliefs and customs of a society or people

ethnic group people who share a common culture, language and heritage

matchmaker someone who arranges marriages on behalf of the bride and groom's family

monsoon season of heavy rain

plateau large, flat area found in higher regions

rickshaw small passenger vehicle pulled by someone running or riding a bike

INDEX

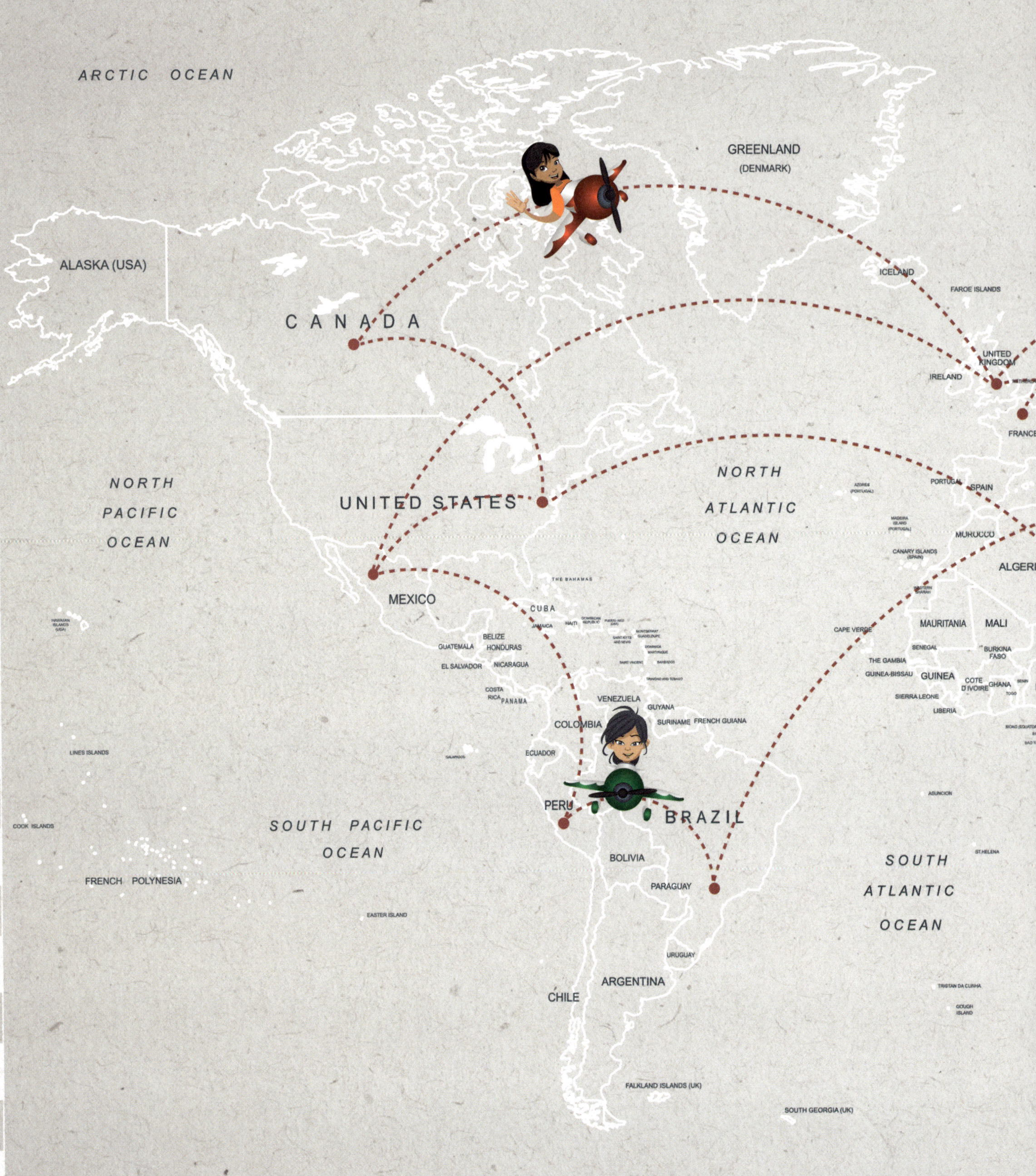

ARCTIC OCEAN
GREENLAND
(DENMARK)
ALASKA (USA)
CANADA
ICELAND
FAROE ISLANDS
UNITED KINGDOM
IRELAND
FRANCE
NORTH PACIFIC OCEAN
UNITED STATES
NORTH ATLANTIC OCEAN
PORTUGAL
SPAIN
MOROCCO
ALGERIA
MEXICO
THE BAHAMAS
CUBA
JAMAICA
HAITI
BELIZE
GUATEMALA
HONDURAS
EL SALVADOR
NICARAGUA
COSTA RICA
PANAMA
CAPE VERDE
MAURITANIA
MALI
SENEGAL
BURKINA FASO
THE GAMBIA
GUINEA-BISSAU
GUINEA
COTE D'IVOIRE
GHANA
SIERRA LEONE
LIBERIA
VENEZUELA
GUYANA
SURINAME
FRENCH GUIANA
COLOMBIA
ECUADOR
LINES ISLANDS
PERU
BRAZIL
SOUTH PACIFIC OCEAN
COOK ISLANDS
FRENCH POLYNESIA
BOLIVIA
PARAGUAY
SOUTH ATLANTIC OCEAN
EASTER ISLAND
URUGUAY
ARGENTINA
CHILE
FALKLAND ISLANDS (UK)
SOUTH GEORGIA (UK)